# LIFTING THE
# VEILS

POCKET EDITION

Published from
Mardukite Borsippa HQ, San Luis Valley, Colorado
Mardukite Academy & Systemology Society
*for spiritual or educational purposes only*

# LIFTING THE VEILS

## Systemology
## Professional Course
## Booklet #10

Developed by Joshua Free
for the Systemology Society

THE JOSHUA FREE IMPRINT
JFI PUBLICATIONS

© 2023, JOSHUA FREE

ISBN : 978-1-961509-35-1

Pocket Paperback Edition — *December 2023*

**mardukite.com**

## Chart Your Flight For Ascension...
### Then Let Your Spirit Fly!

Unlock your ultimate spiritual potential by removing barriers to your true native state.

Learn how to easily attain Self-actualization and help to actualize others along the way.

A greater appreciation and understanding of *Spiritual Life* and *Existence* awaits you. Expand your reach to achieve your dreams.

Each 'Professional Course' lesson-booklet offers simple exercises and techniques that directly apply the philosophy of Systemology, assisting to increase your true knowingness, improve your capabilities in this life, and even decide what you will do in your next.

At the Mardukite Academy of Systemology, the 'Professional Course' lessons in this series are presented to Seeker's that have already completed the 'Basic Course', previously released as six lesson-booklets, or the six-in-one single volume edition "Fundamentals of Systemology."

This all new presentation of the Systemology 'Pathway-to-Ascension' takes Seekers and continuing students from "Zero" to "Infinity" at lightning-fast speeds!

### Discover Who You Really Are...
### Because You Were Never Human

<u>Fundamentals of Systemology</u>
Basic Course Lesson Booklet Series

#1 – *Being More Than Human*
#2 – *Realities In Agreement*
#3 – *Windows To Experience*
#4 – *Ancient Systemology*
#5 – *A History of Systemology*
#6 – *Systemology Processing*


<u>The Pathway to Ascension</u>
Professional Course Lesson Booklet Series

#1 – *Increasing Awareness*
#2 – *Thought & Emotion*
#3 – *Clear Communication*
#4 – *Handling Humanity*
#5 – *Free Your Spirit*
#6 – *Escaping Spirit-Traps*
#7 – *Eliminating Barriers*
#8 – *Conquest of Illusion*
#9 – *Confronting the Past*
#10 – *Lifting the Veils*
#11 – *Spiritual Implants*

*...more titles in this series coming soon!*

# TABLET OF CONTENTS

COURSE INTRODUCTION

– Welcome, Seeker! . . . 11
– A New View of the Human Spirit . . . 13
– Studying the Professional Course . . . 17
– Charting a Course on the Pathway . . . 22
– Taking Flight on the Pathway . . . 25

LESSON TEN:
LIFTING THE VEILS

– Spiritual Beingness . . . 33
– "Locational" Processing . . . 36
– "Creation" and "Knowingness" . . . 42
– "Metaspiritual" Systemology . . . 47
– "Metauniversal" Systemology . . . 54
– Spiritual Energy and Beams . . . 58
– "ZU-Vision" and Perception . . . 64

APPENDIX

– Glossary . . . 75
– Additional Resources . . . 93

# PROFESSIONAL
# COURSE
# INTRODUCTION

## WELCOME, SEEKER!
## LET'S CHART YOUR JOURNEY
## ON THE PATHWAY

*Systemology* is a "holistic" approach to understanding the human experience. It is not actually a singular "subject" in itself, but rather, a new way in which to view the many subjects of *Life* and all *Existence.*

This is a professional course in *Systemology*—specifically, how to *apply* the spiritual philosophy of *Mardukite Systemology* as a personal *"Pathway"* to *Ascension.* Our *Systemology* is a new approach to *"Self-Actualization."* It is completely relevant for the modern age and the future; and quite different from any previous similar attempts, or other traditions, you might find. What's more: it is applicable to anyone with any background.

This *"Professional Course"* series of lessons (booklets) immediately follows the material given in the *"Basic Course"* series—available as six separate pocket-sized booklets, or in a single hardcover volume titled: *"Fundamentals of Systemology: A New Thought For The 21st Century."*

This is a *new* presentation of *Systemology*, emphasizing the application of our philosophy for those *Seekers* that are *"Flying-Solo"*—or else working through their studies and exercises as solitary practitioners. This is a new innovation for *Systemology*. Aside from the book *"Crystal Clear,"* all of our former advanced courses have placed a focus on *"Traditional Piloting"*—where experienced practitioners assist *Seekers* in *"processing."*

To receive the greatest benefit from this study: it is expected that a *Seeker* will already be familiar with the fundamental concepts and terminology (previously relayed in the *Basic Course*) before using lessons from the *Professional Course*. This will allow us to cover the extensive territory of the *Pathway* much more quickly. However, for reference, a basic "*glossary*" of vocabulary used in this lesson is provided in the "*appendix*."

---

## A NEW VIEW OF THE HUMAN SPIRIT

*Systemology* is not a religion and does not require any type of *faith*. It is, however, built upon a "spiritual" premise—and as such is an "applied spiritual philosophy." It is based on ancient teachings that we are *Spiritual Beings* essentially "wearing" bodies like clothes—or using them as "vehicles." Yet our true native nature is not *physical*, but beyond this existence; and we can certainly operate a "body" from *outside* of it.

We are **all** *Spiritual Beings*—each of us a *unit* of *Spiritual Awareness*—that have experienced a very long *Spiritual Timeline* of existence. Although we might be particularly attached to the familiar "physical shells" associated with *this* lifetime, our true *"Spiritual Lifetime"* is seemingly *eternal*. We have been many things before *Human*, and we go onward as a *Spiritual Being* after our *"genetic vehicle"* of *this* incarnation perishes.

While a "spiritual" view of the *Human Condition* may not seem unique to our philosophy, just how often is the concept treated *systematically*? For that matter: just how many people, supposedly raised to this or that religion, or professing to believe one thing or another, actually live their lives as though they are *Spirits?*

As *Spiritual Beings* of immortal existence and infinite potential, we are not simply the *"creations"* of an even greater *Being-*

*ness*; we are, in fact, an integral part of that *"creative force"* which permeates all existence.

Our basic nature is to be a *"creative being"* — our highest goals are *"to create."* And as such a being — which we refer to as an *Alpha-Spirit* in *Systemology* — we have run into some difficulties along the course of our *Spiritual Timeline* and found ourselves trapped within material *Universes* of our own collaborative *creation*.

Since we did not start out our existence in a trapped condition, it is correct to say that we have *"fallen"* from our native *"godlike"* states. It did not happen all at one, but progressively and systematically. We know our "troubles" have resulted from accumulated "barriers" and "blockages" — or *fragmentation* — during our vast experiences as *Spiritual Beings*. They are not because we lack something; but because of what's been added.

In *Systemology*, we systematically examine those routes by which we must have descended to reach our present condition, then reverse the direction of travel and chart a personal "*Pathway to Ascension.*" Of course, the exact "details" of the *Spiritual Timeline* will be different for each individual *Seeker*. However, we have been able to systematically chart our *Pathway* based on common patterns of *Human fragmentation*.

In the most basic terms: the *fragmentation* that defines our "downward spiral" consists of decisions or considerations where we deny our true nature. This includes those decisions to "*withdraw*" rather than "*reach*"; where we choose to *not-know* rather than *know*; to *not-communicate* rather than *communicate*; and ultimately, to take *no-responsibility* for being a *creative-cause*, and therefore succumb to being an *effect*.

But there is *hope!* And much more importantly: there is an effectively workable *way out* of the mazes and traps of our existence. If you are reading this now, you have already begun to gather your tools and build up the *"horsepower"* necessary to break the gravity holding your *Spiritual Beingness* to the *Human Condition.*

---

## STUDYING THE
## PROFESSIONAL COURSE

Most *Seekers* study and practice *Systemology* at-a-distance and independent of the "Mardukite Academy" or any "Master-level" mentors trained therein. This means that the *books* (and to a lesser degree, the *internet*) are the only means of direct contact a *Seeker* maintains with the "Systemology Society" during their studies. A continuing *Seeker* from the *"Basic Course"* will be familiar with the style of study found in *this* course.

Misunderstood words are the most common reason an individual abandons studying a subject. When a misunderstanding occurs, *Awareness* declines. These misunderstandings start to "stack up" after the first occurrence, and as a result, the level of interest and attention will also decline. This is how a "confusion" develops; and the individual will get "bored" with the subject, feel tired, and unable to concentrate.

One solution is to return to the part of the material that was still interesting and enjoyable to read. When scanning around that area of text, there is likely to be a new word (or new specific use of a familiar word) that is unclear, but was passed by unnoticed. All *Systemology* books include their own *glossary*. Using this *glossary* and a high-quality dictionary will help resolve this misunderstanding once it is located.

An effective education of any subject is taught on a *gradient*. This is what is intended by presenting the study of something as "*grades*." Rather than treating a subject as one total mass, true learning is achieved by increasing one's understanding with a *gradual* increase upward. The *ascent* to a mountaintop is not successfully achieved in one leap, but by targeting and reaching specific checkpoints along the way.

This *Professional Course* consists of a series of lessons (booklets) that gradually increase a *Seeker's* ability to understand and apply the practices and techniques of *Systemology* as a complete "*Pathway to Ascension*." It is an appropriate study for continuing *Seekers* (from the *Basic Course*), but also "advanced" *Systemologists*.

Each lesson (booklet) of the *Professional Course* applies *Systemology* to a particular subject (or focus). It is best if the entire course can be studied and applied in sequential order. These lessons also employ a style of practice or technique called "*Systematic Processing.*" An introduction to applying this methodology is provided in the final lesson (booklet) of the *Basic Course*—or in the "*Fundamentals of Systemology*" volume.

To study the *Professional Course* just like a student at the Academy: a *Seeker* reads through all instructional material and applies each exercise (or "*process*") presented in the text to the extent they comfortably can, before continuing on to the next lesson (booklet).

When first starting on the *Pathway* as a *Solo* practitioner, without the aid of an experienced *Pilot*, a *Seeker* shouldn't "push too hard" or allow themselves to get too "stuck" on any one area (lesson) or *process*. It is not expected that any one area will be completely handled when first introduced. For optimum results, it is expected that a serious *Seeker* will make more than one "pass" through the entire *Professional Course.*

The *Professional Course* is not altogether different from other forms of practical or technical education: where the instruction and exercises are delivered to a completion, and then a student further increases their abilities, strength and skill-level by applying additional practice throughout their life. Therefore, a student should not concern themselves with perfectly mastering each step (or lesson) before progressing forward.

Additional passes through the material are likely to result in different *"realizations"* (an increased *level of understanding*) than a previous time. New "layers" of *Knowingness* may now be accessible during a *process* that may not have been before. It is important to avoid invalidating the progress you've made just because one area is not completely handled right away, or if a certain *process* seems too difficult on the first pass.

## CHARTING A COURSE ON THE PATHWAY

Although we can communicate a systematic structure to *fragmentation,* the personal journey experienced along the *Pathway* will be different for each *Seeker.* For example, certain areas will seem more *"turbulent"* or difficult for one *Seeker* than another. We tend to say that these areas have more *"charge"* on them—or that they are more *"heavily charged."* It is best to handle such areas when you are already feeling "good" and not in a situation (or condition) where that specific area is consistently being *"triggered"* or *"restimulated."*

As an applied philosophy, *Systemology* "theory" can be easily utilized in the "laboratory" of the "world-at-large" in everyday life. This is implied within the basic instruction of each lesson. Unlike other "sciences" that conduct experiments by making a change to some "objective variable" *out there* and waiting to see an effect, our focus is the individual (or *Observer*) themselves, and how *they* affect the "*Reality*" perceived.

In addition to applying *Systemology* "New Thought" to everyday life, our philosophy is applied by using specific exercises and systematic techniques. These "*processes*" provide the most stable personal gain (and *realizations*) for each area; but only when actually applied with a *Seeker's* full "*presence*" and *Awareness*.

This *Professional Course* is designed so that it may be easily read and studied with little concern for what "dangers" these teachings—or *processing*—might unleash. However, there are still some guidelines that pertain to the "best-uses" of these course lessons, particularly if a *Seeker* intends for stable development.

Skipping over too much material/*processing* in early lessons may make attempts to understand (or apply) later lessons more difficult. However, once the complete *Professional Course* is worked through at least once in its entirety, specific areas can then be later returned to and treated with a greater sense of *Awareness* and *"presence"* than before. Of course, in *"Traditional Piloting,"* the rate of processing is monitored by an experienced practitioner; but in *"Solo-Processing,"* a *Seeker* must regulate their own progress on the *Pathway*.

Applying a systematic technique is called *"running a process."* The *processes* are designed with very simple instructions or "command-lines." To *run* a *processing command-line*, a *Seeker* may be assisted by the communication of that *line* from a "Co-Pilot" (as in "Traditional Piloting"). But even then, a *Seeker* must still personally "input" the *command* as *Self.* For this reason —and quite thankfully— *Solo-Processing* is possible.

---

## TAKING FLIGHT ON THE PATHWAY

*Processing Techniques* are intended to treat the *Spiritual Being* or *Alpha-Spirit*; the individual themselves. It is applied by the *Alpha-Spirit*—then *Self-directed* to the "Mind-System" or even a "body" (*genetic-vehicle*), both of which are "constructs" that the *Alpha-Spirit* (*Self*, or the "I-AM" *Awareness unit*) operates, but neither of which is actually *Self. Fragmentation* causes *Humans* to falsely identify *Self as* the "*Mind*" or even a "*Body.*"

The *Professional Course* lessons (booklets) are designed for the *Beginning Seeker* in mind—one that may have an understanding of theory, but with little experience in practice. That being said: each of these lessons may be used toward total *Beta-Defragmentation* within a specific area. There are also more *processes* given for each subject than may be necessary to achieve an *ultimate end-point realization* on that entire area.

Some *processes* can be treated quite lightly at first; others may require a bit of working at in order to get *"running"* well. It is important to set aside a period of time when you can be dedicated to your studies and *processing.* This period of time is referred to as a *"processing session."* The reason for this, is that when a *process* does start *running* well, it is important to be able to complete it to a satisfactory *"end-point."*

The purpose of *systematic processing* is to be able to *really* "look" at things and even determine the *considerations* we have made—or attitudes we have decided—about *Reality* as a result of those experiences. It doesn't do us much good to simply "glance"—or to *restimulate* something uncomfortable and then quickly *withdraw* from it once again, leaving more of our *attention* yet again behind and held fixedly on it.

Generally speaking, a *Seeker* continues to *run* a *process* so long as something is "happening"—which is to say, the *process* is still producing a change. Usually this is evident by the type of "answers" that a *command-line* helps a *Seeker* originate from the database of their own *Mind-System*. The *command-lines* do not "do" anything on their own. They assist a *Seeker* to direct their own attention toward increasing *Awareness*.

Of course, a *Seeker* may also cease to generate new "data" from a *process* without reaching an *"ultimate" realization* as an *"end-point."* It is possible that additional "layers" (or even other "areas") require handling before anything "deeper" is accessible. If this is the case, end the *process*. But, if a *Seeker* is *withdrawing* from something uncomfortable that was incited or stirred up, then a *process* is *run* until they feel "good" about it.

In case the thought of encountering *"turbulence"* is a concern: the techniques given as *"Opening Procedures"* of a *Formal Session* (in the *Basic Course*), and those found in the earliest lessons of the *Professional Course*, are quite useful when applied as "safety nets" for maintaining *Awareness* and *presence*, even when *Flying-Solo*.

One of the benefits to *Flying-Solo* is that *processing* is entirely *Self-determined*. This already provides a certain built-in "safety" for a practitioner. Anything you *restimulate* by *Self-determinism* is *your thing*. It is not incited by external *other-determined* influences (or other "source-points" in existence) that make you an *effect*. It can be more easily handled in *processing*—or you can simply let things "cool down" and come back to it again.

While it may seem "mysterious" to beginners, a *Seeker* gets a sense for knowing how long to *run* a *process* only with practice. Once you have spent some time actually applying the *Professional Course*, there are many aspects that become "second nature" because they are, in fact, a part of our true original nature. All we have done is *"reverse engineer"* the routes of *creation* and *consideration* that are already *our own*.

# LESSON TEN:
# LIFTING
# THE VEILS

## SPIRITUAL BEINGNESS

In addition to gaining greater *control* over the *"Mind-Body"* systems inherent in the experience of the *"Human Condition,"* a *Seeker* will also have increased their *Awareness* on the *truth* of *Being* an *Alpha-Spirit* that is *having* a *Human* experience—and we now continue further in this area for *Systemology Level-4.*

Previously in these *Professional Course* lessons, we began suggesting the idea that an individual, in their native state, is an *Alpha-Spirit*—a unit of *Spiritual Awareness* that is not, itself, actually located in *this Physical Universe* (*Beta-Existence*).

Of course, the *Alpha-Spirit* can *think* or *consider* that it is located in *space-time*; and it can also *think* that it *must only* operate from the specific *viewpoint* of the place it *thinks* it's located.

An *Alpha-Spirit* is without "form" or "mass." It is *Pure Awareness*. In order to experience "*pain*" (and therefore a potential "*loss*" of a *Body*) an *Alpha-Spirit* must "*postulate*" or "*strongly consider*" its own *Beingness* as one-and-the-same with a *Body*; by this, we mean to fully "*identify*" *Self* with a *Body*.

*At* basic, we cannot actually be "harmed," but once we *consider* that we *must have* a *Body*, then the *fragmentation* about "*losing*" a *Body* follows shortly thereafter. Once an *Alpha-Spirit creates* (or *projects*) *energy-matter* (by *intention* and *attention*) to operate in a fixed position (*identifying Self* and establishing a sense of *ownership* there), the *Being* (as a *Spiritual Awareness*) can now be "located" in that position—thus it can be "harmed" (or "hit") in that position. Of course, eventually that position deteriorates (or is "smashed"/"collapses") and they must establish a new position to operate from.

As this pattern of activity continues, much of an individual's own history (*Spiritual Timeline* or *Backtrack*) consists of "abandoning unsafe" or collapsed locations and frequently "leaving stuff" behind. This systematically weakens the *spiritual power* of the *Being*, because the native ability to *have* and *create* "*space*" is governed by the ability and willingness to *reach*—in this case, to literally "*knowingly reach*" rather than "*reactively withdraw*" from *locations*. In this regard, we are really speaking about two distinct *levels* of *existence*—*Beta* and *Alpha*.

There is, of course, the *Physical Universe* (*Beta-Existence*). An *Alpha-Spirit withdraws* from those "unpleasant locations" and "painful positions" until they can no longer operate outside (or apart from) a *Body*. Then, there is the individual's own *Personal Universe* (or *Alpha* state), which includes what some refer to as the "*mental universe*" equivalent of *space-time energy-matter*.

The term *"mental"* is not systematically appropriate for our purposes. Often, the term is meant to simply mean "non-physical" or "metaphysical," but we prefer to define the *"mental universe"* as part of an *Alpha* or *Spiritual Existence*—one that is composed of the *Alpha-Spirit's* own *creations*, in contrast to the *shared creations* of a *Shared Universe* (or *Beta-Existence*).

## "LOCATIONAL" PROCESSING

On a higher *Alpha* level ("higher" than what we perceive with the *Human Condition*), the *Alpha-Spirit* is operating from a fixed location in its own *Personal Universe* along with the *"controls"* and *"systems"* for experiencing *Beta-Existence*. In the "video game" of *Life*, the "controls" and "system hardware" are not elements experienced directly as part of the *game* that is appearing displayed on the *screen*.

These elements are *exterior* (and in many ways "superior") to the more apparent *Game Universe* that is being experienced from an *interior viewpoint*.

We focus primarily on *Beta-Defragmentation* in our course instruction, because the truth is that many of the cycles, tendencies, behaviors and patterns that are observably exhibited in *this* lifetime and *this Universe* are indicative of the same type of things we find further and earlier on the *Backtrack*. The same *fragmented mechanisms* involved (or attached) with *withdrawing* from *unsafe locations* in *Beta-Existence*, also applies to what is taking place (at an *Alpha* level) regarding an individual's own *Personal Universe*. As the *Arcane Tablets* from both *Mesopotamia* and *Hermetic Traditions* relay: *"As Above; So Below."*

In *running* the following *processes*, simply *consider* whatever "comes up" or "feels right." The *locations* indicated in these *processing command-lines* ("PCL") do not have to be restricted to *this Existence,* though a *Seeker* is likely to start with answers that are relatively closer or more familiar. As an individual stops *compulsively withdrawing* from *occupied locations,* more *spiritual ability* comes back under their *control.* This *systematic processing* can be taken much further on additional passes through the *Professional Course*—but initially it may be applied lightly when first introduced to this *processing level.*

For each of the following PCL, *spot* many *locations*—and allow for the one's that may not make sense (or seem rational) to come up as well.

A. *"Spot some places where you would be safe."*

B. *"Spot some places where a parent (or guardian) would be safe."*

C. *"Spot some places where a child would be safe."*

D. *"Spot some places where a lover (or companion) would be safe."*

E. *"Spot some places where a teacher (or leader) would be safe."*

F. *"Spot some places where lifeforms would be safe."*

G. *"Spot some places where valuable belongings would be safe."*

H. *"Spot some places where energy would be safe."*

I. *"Spot some places where ideas would be safe."*

J. *"Spot some places where a spirit would be safe."*

K. *"Spot some places where it would be safe to keep a god."*

The following PCL-formula concerns *communicating* an *intention* or *control* to a particular *"part of the body"* as a general *process*. There are other applications of this too—such as to assist *attention* in managing "pain" or "difficulties" with a particular *"part of the body."* A *Seeker* will likely start with "physical locations" as their answers, but as an advanced practice, they should try to work up to *considering* the locations within their *Personal Universe.*

This PCL is a formula that is used for multiple *processes* by inserting different "terminals" into the blank space.

First start with *"bodies,"* using the terminals: "HAND"; "FOOT"; "STOMACH"; "GENITALS"; "HEAD"; "EYES"; "EARS"; and "BRAIN."

Then use terminals for *"roles/identities,"* such as: "LOVED ONE"; "AUTHORITY FIGURE"; "ANGRY/EMOTIONAL PERSON"; "DANGEROUS CREATURE"; "VICTIM"; and "GOD."

The PCL-formula is:

*"From where could you communicate to (a) ---?"*

Now, regardless of how many PCL you used (or how many answers you came up with) for the *locational processes* given previously (in this section), *run* the following two in *alternation* a few times.

A. *"Spot some places you are willing to be."*

B. *"Spot some places you are willing to not be."*

Our final set of *processes* for this section involves another PCL-formula. This time we will apply it to *"concepts"* rather than *"terminals"* (with mass). The PCL uses the word *"create"* to mean everything from lightly imagined *visualizations*, to vivid *mental images*, to really manifesting something in *Beta-Existence*.

The PCL-formula is:

*"From where could you create ---?"*

First start with some basic concepts: "A PICTURE"; "AN EMOTION"; "A MENTAL MACHINE"; "AN AUTOMATED REACT-

ION"; "FRAGMENTED CHARGE"; "A PAINFUL FEELING"; and "A MIND."

Then, apply some of these advanced concepts (or wait until a second pass through this course): "BEING TRICKED"; "TRICK-ING ANOTHER"; "BEING ABUSED"; "AB-USING ANOTHER"; "BEING BETRAYED"; "BETRAYING ANOTHER"; "BEING TRAPPED"; "TRAPPING ANOTHER"; "A GAME"; "AN IDENTITY"; "AN OBJECT"; and "A REALITY."

---

## CREATION AND KNOWINGNESS

At the top of the *Alpha* "scale" of *Existence*, there is only "*Creation*." Whereas the goal of *Beta-Existence* (or a *Games Universe*) may be "*Survival*," in our true native *god-like* state, our *Alpha* purpose is solely "*To Create*." Even at a *Human* level, the act of "*creating*" is incredibly satisfying and desirable. But this is not the only *state* or *condition* that is available to (or able to be experienced by) a *god-like Alpha-Spirit*.

The *Alpha* state of "*Creation*" includes a level of *Knowingness* that extends far beyond simply "*knowing about*" something. It is an "all-pervasive" (nearly absolute) type of *Knowingness* concerning our own *creations*. But, as *god-like Eternal Beings*, this state does not provide us with much in terms of "*games*." When we *know-all* and *see-all*, there is no "randomness" or "chance" possible for us to experience—there is no "*game*."

As *Spiritual Beings* with a near-*infinite* existence, maintaining a position at the very top of the *Alpha* scale became "boring." We wanted to also be able to "*go into*" our *Creations* and "*play*"—to be able to actually experience our *Creations*. As such, we developed a specialized type of "*Not-Knowing*" that could be practiced from our *god-like* state in order to make our ex-

43

perience of existence—our experience of our *Creations*—"more interesting." This works out just fine until we find ourselves with a bunch of *rigidly fixed Not-Knows* that are now outside of our *control*.

Therefore, just below "*Creation*" (at the top of our *Alpha* scale) we have a specialized state of "*Not-Know.*" This, at least initially, is *Self-Determined* (as a "*postulate*" or *Alpha-Thought*) to intentionally "block out" the perfect *Knowingness* (that one begins with as *Creator*) in order to make experience of "*games*" possible—in which we now have something to "*Know-About*" or "*find out about.*" The scale further continues gradually downward—but in this lesson, we are not concerned with "scraping the bottom."

The following *processing exercises* help a *Seeker* get more perspective on this area by *knowingly* practicing it—even if only conceptually. In *running* these: you can

"*Not-Know*" something that you really *do* know, something you *don't* know, or even something you are *unsure* of. For example: with "*objects*," you might already know how much it weighs, but in practice, decide you don't; or perhaps you might really not know anything about when it was made, and provide that as an answer. You can "*Not-Know*" (*Step-B*) many things about a particular "*terminal*" within the same *process*. These practices are intended more for educational purposes than to reach a specific *end-point*.

NOT-KNOWING: OBJECTIVE

A. "*Look around the room and spot an object.*"

B. "*Decide to 'Not-Know' something about it.*"

NOT-KNOWING: POPULATED AREAS

A. "*Look around and spot a person.*"

B. "*Decide to 'Not-Know' something about them.*"

## NOT-KNOWING: ZU-VISION

A. *"Close your eyes; Spot individual things (that might be) in the room."*

B. *"Decide to 'Not-Know' how they look."*

The previous *process* (above) is an advanced practice that *may* help improve *"ZU-Vision"* perceptions (*exterior to the Body*). This *process* is effective because, from within the *Human Condition*, you are already *"Not-Knowing"* how things appear in *Beta-Existence* unless the *Body's Eyes* provide you this sensory information. This is, of course, not true for the actual abilities of the *Alpha-Spirit*, but it is really how things are (or seem) when operating from within fixed *viewpoints "interior to"* the *Human Condition* (or *Body*).

## NOT-KNOWING: CREATION

A. *"Create a mental image of an object."*

B. *"Decide to 'Not-Know' who created it."*

And finally, whenever *running* *"Not-Know,"* even if only in conceptual practice, it is best to *end-session* with actual *re-call processing* (of something *Known*). Therefore, you can complete this area by: selecting something that you can easily remember (such as your favorite food); then alternately decide to "*Know*" and "*Not-Know*" it a few times. Then select something else and repeat this.

---

## METASPIRITUAL SYSTEMOLOGY

Experience of the physics and material knowledge of *Beta-Existence* is only one part of what we may apply *Systemology* to. At this point on the *Pathway*, it should be obvious that an individual is much more than just a *Body*—and even the *Mind-System* is "metaphysical," far beyond the scope and reach of "neural-brain sciences." Some of this lesson is based on material that first appeared in a volume of our *Systemology Core*, titled: "*Imaginomicon.*"

The *spiritual side* of *Systemology* offers a *Seeker* more "substance" than what is found in any *religious tradition* or style of *mysticism*. As many *Seekers* (with previous backgrounds with these other methods) have found, our *Systemology* is also far more effective for increasing and/or rehabilitating our true *Spiritual Awareness*. Of course, this does not occur all at once; and it often requires handling our experience of *Beta-Existence* first.

An *Alpha-Spirit* is not simply operating a *Beta-Body* in this *Physical Universe* from its native *Alpha* state. To say so is an oversimplification. The experience of *this* version of *Beta-Existence* has such "apparent solidity" to it because it is the "accumulation," "compactification," and/or "condensation" of all the former versions of *Beta-Existence* (*Universes*) that have since "collapsed" into *this* one—a sort of "common denominator."

The *Alpha-Spirit* also does not "directly"

experience the *Human Condition*. The *"communication"* of that experience—and its *control* by an *Alpha-Spirit*—is filtered and relayed through many levels of *metaphysical or "mental" machinery, energetic fields and beams,* and various layers of *"subtle"* or *"astral"* bodies, all of which remains *continuously created* and *actively running* in the present (from use in previous existences), though the individual has become so entrapped by the *Human Condition* that they are no longer aware of this.

Therefore, what we would *consider* an *"appropriate"* *Body* for the *Alpha-Spirit* in this *Beta-Existence* is also a "condensation" or "greater solidification" of former similar *considerations*. What is maintained from "previous bodies" (existences) *"collapses-in"* on the *Human Body*. We use the expression *"entrapped by"* to be less *restimulative* (of *fragmentation*), but it is more systematically correct to say that the "layers" and "levels" of *Awareness* (and *energetic-stuff*) maintained by an *Alpha-Spirit* (as its own perceived *identity*) progressively "*collapses in*" on the *Human Body/ Condition* for various reasons (for example, when trying to "protect the body" from danger/loss).

Ideally, to *control* a *Body*, an *Alpha-Spirit* would remain entirely *exterior* to it— simply extending a *reach inside* using *intention* (and/or *energy-beams*) to operate one. In its native (*unfragmented*) state, the *Alpha-Spirit* maintains most of its "*energetic-machinery*" completely outside of a *Beta-Existence* in order to keep it from getting too mixed up with *energy-fields* and *reactive-systems* specific to the *Body* (or "*genetic-vehicle*" operated in *Beta-Existence*).

But, again: various circumstances cause *Awareness* to "*collapse in*" or "*snap-in*" on the *Body*—and the *Alpha-Spirit* begins to associate *Self* with a *Body* more and more until their *viewpoint* tends to be "*inside it,*" because the individual believes they *are* it. The "*snap-in*" effects tend to be *energetically turbulent*, which causes a type of *fragmentation* that inhibits an individual from "*ZU-Vision*" (or "*spiritual sight,*" where an *Alpha-Spirit* is not dependent on sensory perception from within the *Human Condition*).

The *Alpha-Spirit* began "*outside*" (or "*exterior to*") *Beta-Existence*—and any associated *genetic-vehicles*—prior to being "*snapped-in*" to it. This is the first area that requires *defragmenting* in order to lift some of the veils that distort our *clear view* as *Alpha-Spirits*. For this, we directly apply to this area the *systematic processing techniques* a *Seeker* has already developed proficiency with throughout this *Professional Course*.

To begin, we will provide a list of *keywords* (or "*buttons*") and a basic *processing-structure* (or *formula*). We are targeting any incidents that relate to "*going interior*" in some way, in order to *relieve* some of the *fragmentation* attached to *automatic/reactive* "*snap-in*" effects. Select one of the *keywords* from the list that seems the most interesting—and once that is *run* well, choose another to *process* until you "feel good" in regards to this area.

The *keywords* are: "GO IN"; "PUT IN"; "WANT TO GO IN"; "MUST GET IN"; "CAN'T GET IN"; "KICKED OUT"; "BE TRAPPED"; "FORCED IN"; "PULLED IN"; and "PUSHED IN."

In *Traditional Piloting*, the language structure of a PCL is easily modified *in-session* to apply to various lists such as these. A *Seeker* will notice that the following *processing-structure* is worded to apply to, for example, the first, second, and third *keyword* on the list, but would not make sense for some of the others. For *Solo-Piloting* a *Seeker* should write out the proper

PCL for a specific *process before running it*, if it does not fit the *structure-formula* as printed in the lesson. [For example: *"have the feeling or sense that you must get in."*]

1. *"Recall making someone ---."*

2. *"Recall being made to ---."*

3. *"Recall someone making another ---."*

0. *"Recall a time when you decided to ---."*

If any of these *"buttons"* seem particularly *"charged"* or *"turbulent"* (and do not seem to be *defragmenting* with *Analytical Recall*), use the techniques and training from the previous lesson (*"Confronting the Past"*) to *run* the *"chain-of-incidents"* or *"chain-of-fragmentation"* that is holding up (or suspending) *Awareness* in that area. The *"chain"* is typically specific to *one* of the four *"circuit-types"* treated in the *process* (above). [If necessary, a *Seeker* may also run a PCL using *"imagine"* in place of *"recall."*]

## METAUNIVERSAL SYSTEMOLOGY

In addition to the *"snap-in"* effects generally associated with an *Alpha-Spirit's* own *Awareness* regarding a *Body*, there is a similar area of *fragmentation* attached to *"collapse-of-space."* By this, we mean literally the phenomenon of *"energy fields"* and *"space"* collapsing-in-on the *Alpha-Spirit*.

At the upper-most levels of our *Systemological Philosophy*, the *"collapse-of-space"* phenomenon is most strongly tied to experiencing the *"Collapse-of-a-Universe."* As one might guess, this is a very *turbulent* area of *spiritual fragmentation*. The magnitude of potential *"loss"* or *"sadness"* connected to this area far exceeds anything an individual is likely to newly experience in *this* lifetime. But as with other areas of *fragmentation*, there are everyday situations where this might even become *restimulated.*

This area represents some of the earliest *fragmentation* we have ever experienced — and it is innate to each and every one of us. The first time it was strongly *imprinted* is during the original *collapse-of* the *Alpha-Spirit's* personal and individual *"Home Universe."* Since then, there have, of course, been other experiences that later reinforced the *fragmentation* to a point where the individual no longer is *willing* to be personally *responsible* for *"Creation-of-Space."*

This present lesson is, in many ways, a direct continuance of the *"Locational Processing"* and *"Creation-of-Space"* exercises introduced in *Lesson-5 ("Free Your Spirit")* —and elsewhere, in our *"Imaginomicon."* These previous exercises depicted the basic structure of *space* (or a *Universe*) as a *"cube"* —defined by *eight* *"corner-points"* that *"anchor"* the boundaries (or dimensions) of that *space*. An *Alpha-Spirit* maintains *"anchor-points"* that they use to define their own personal perception of *space/creation*.

Just as there are experiences of one's own *point-of-view* ("POV") *"snapping-in"* on a new *"plane"* of *space,* or a new *"mass"* (or *"Body"*), so too are there *imprints* of when *space* and *energy-matter*—and the very *"corners"* or *"anchor-points"* of a *Universe* itself—*"collapse-in"* on the individual. This area is *defragmented* similarly to the *systematic processing* from the previous section (above). Essentially, a *Seeker* is looking to *run* this area as *incidents*, using their training and experience with procedures in this and previous lessons. We are targeting different *incidents* than before. Rather than a *viewpoint* ("POV") being *snapped-in* on some *space* or *mass*, the reverse is *processed*.

The *"hot buttons"* (or *keywords* or *phrases*) used for *defragmenting* this area include:

*incidents* of *space collapsing-in* on the POV; the world *closing-in* or *folding-up*; *energy imploding* or *collapsing-in* on the POV; *corner-points collapsing-in* or *snapping-in* on the POV; sudden *"uncreation"* or *folding-up* of all *forms/space*; the environment/*space caving-in* on the POV; being *pulled back* from; *falling away* from; and the *sense* that everything is suddenly becoming *unreal*.

Handling this area properly may be too advanced of a step for some *Seekers* on their first pass through materials of the *Professional Course*; get what you can from it and spend more time in this area when you come back to it. As an additional note from the *upper-levels* of *realization*: it is always the *Alpha-Spirit* themselves that *collapses* their own *space*. Although environmental stimuli and pressure (or trickery) from others may get you to do it, you are the only one that can actually *snap-in* your own *"anchor-points."*

## SPIRITUAL ENERGY & BEAMS

In the beginning, an *Alpha-Spirit* operated on pure *Alpha-Thought* and *"postulates"* — *creating* things and making things *just happen* by *intention* alone. But below this level, as we began to *Share Universes* with others, we made *reality-agreements* concerning the necessity of using *energy* to *create* and *change* things.

In terms of the *Human Condition*, or the operation of a *"genetic-vehicle,"* the *Alpha-Spirit* tends to direct *energy-beams* into the head, into the back of the neck, into various spots up and down the spine, and the *"solar plexus"* or stomach region. There is also the tendency to wrap a long coil-like beam around the mid-section (or torso), which can then be used to abruptly *pull* the body from perceived danger.

When operating a *Body* using *energy-*

*beams* while *"exterior to"* it, there isn't much "kick-back" from the *Body* since everything is handled remotely. If, however, one's own POV is fixedly *"interior to"* the *Body*, then even the presence or impact of these *energy-beams* alone can produce intermittent or sporadic headache sensations and stomach discomfort, *&tc.* —an entire variety of *"pings"* on our *Awareness* become possible.

Using experience from previous *training levels*, some *Seekers* have learned to provide *"relief"* for these specific types of *"pings"* by determining what the *energy-flow* of the *beam* is, and reversing it; or by repeatedly alternating the *intention* to *increase* and then *reduce* (or *reverse*) it, until it becomes under greater *control*.

Although handling *energy-beams* directly is a more *advanced level* of practice, it is never too early to start *considering* what is *actually* happening with one's own personal *energy* and *Awareness* when various *incidents* occur—or *have occurred*, when *running incident processing.* We have been handling this area *lightly* and somewhat indirectly all throughout the *Professional Course.* This makes *recognizing* it much easier as a *Seeker* progresses further along the *Pathway.*

Since the *Alpha-Spirit* maintains a continuous *Spiritual Timeline* (or *Backtrack*) that extends through many previous *Universes*, it is a reasonable conclusion that we are certainly not limited to a *location* within *this* version of *Beta-Existence.* Of course, without heavy *fragmentation*, we are well more *aware* of this fact—and we *know* that we are *reaching into* our *Creations* and *Games Universes* in order to operate and experience things.

Given that the *Alpha-Spirit's* own actual (*Alpha*) existence is *exterior to* any experienced *Beta-Existence*, it does not have any reason to not operate from an *interior viewpoint* to have a better "*game*" experience. One might even note the sheer increase in *"first-person perspective"* video game popularity in the past few decades.

Although a *god-like* being might, at first, be quite able to operate multiple *"bodies"* or *"games"* simultaneously, eventually more and more *Awareness* *"collapses-in"* on *one* specific *lifeform* or *genetic-vehicle*. By this point, the native *spiritual ability* to simply *"recreate"* a *Body* at will has also diminished. The *Alpha-Spirit* is now able to feel *"loss"* when a *Body* is destroyed — hence the "new-found" *intentions* to *protect* one.

Then, finally, when the *Alpha-Spirit* *"identifies"* or *"associates"* *Self* too closely with the *Body*, experience of *pain* is possible — mainly to give warning about a *potential loss* to (or of) the *Body*. When beings realized how unpleasant it is to occupy the "center" of a *Body*, they created *"control centers"* to operate from that are close to, but stand apart from, the *Body*.

This is only partly what we mean in *Systemology* regarding a *"Master Control Center"* (of the *Alpha-Spirit*) versus a *"Reactive Control Center"* (that is specific to a *Body*). And while the types of *mechanisms* are *"metaphysical"* in nature, they *are "energetic-constructs"* that have *form* or *mass*—and therefore have *"control points"* or *"anchor-points"* that define its nature and the *metaphysical space* it occupies. These *"points"* also have a tendency to *"snap-in"* or *"collapse-in"* on the *Body* during certain *incidents*—and with the type of *effects* or *fragmentation* we have been describing throughout this lesson.

When *running* some of the earliest *incidents* in this area, the *Alpha-Spirit* will still be operating from a point *interior-to* a *Body*, while simultaneously projecting *"operating/control-points"* that are *exterior-to* the *Body* (but placed closely around it for protection). If a *Seeker* doesn't have much *"reality"* yet on this idea, it may be taken up on future passes through the *Professional Course* material. However, the *systematic-sequence* that may be *processed* is (*run*) as follows:

1. *Operating from an "interior" control-point.*

2. *Operating from an "exterior" control-point.*

3. *The "exterior" control-point "collapses-in" to the body.*

As an additional advanced practice for this area: *consider* (or *imagine*) some ways that an *Alpha-Spirit* that does not have a *"Body"* could get "into trouble." See if you can *spot* a *"chain-of-incidents"* to *run* that involves something you came up with for this. So, *Imagine* some ways, pick something that *could* be a part of a particular *chain*, and *run* it. Don't worry about *heavy implants* (or *"conditioning"*) for this *processing level*. If they are run into now, just *"recognize"* that such things *do* exist.

## "ZU-VISION" & PERCEPTION

Increased *Awareness* and *perception* is an inherent part of progressing on the *Pathway*. However, research has suggested that the *fragmentation* associated with *"going interior"* or *"snapping-in"* (as described previously) should be *"processed-out"* prior to placing a direct emphasis on *"ZU-Vision"* or (*"spiritual perception"*). The *fragmentation effects* from the first area prohibit and inhibit development or rehabilitation of the second.

Before completing *Systemology Level-4*, a *Seeker* is presented with a series of *systematic processing* exercises and techniques that directly encourage increasing *perceptions* of *"ZU-Vision"* (or *"Spirit Vision"*)—which is to say, placing emphasis on using *viewpoints* that are *exterior-to* the *Body* (*Human Condition*).

As with the presentation of earlier similar exercises in this course, it is expected that a *Seeker* will initially experience a mixture of *real perception* and *imagination* when first practicing in this area. It is important to not *invalidate* your progress by comparing what is *perceived* in practice with what you might *see* using eyes of the *Body*. The development (or rehabilitation) of *true spiritual ability* occurs gradually.

As a good general "warm-up" for this type of work, repeatedly *alternate* the following PCL with *eyes closed*, until you have *some* degree of certainty regarding your *perception* "*exterior-to*" the *Body*. Some *Seekers* prefer to practice these types of *processes* while lying down. [*Eyes closed; blindfolded if necessary.*]

A. "*Spot three points in the body.*"
B. "*Spot three points in the room.*"

This next *process* is best run outdoors (with *eyes open*). Repeat it many times un-

til you can really get a sense of *"space."*
Once you have some *reality* on the exercise this way, perform the same steps with *eyes closed.*

A. *"Spot two objects."*

B. *"Notice the distance between them."*

C. *"Get a real sense of the 'space' between them."*

There is a very ancient and much misunderstood spiritual practice referred to as *"Journeying to Other Planets"* or *"Traversing the Star-Gates."* In many ways, it is meant to extend a *Seeker's attention* further and further away from the rigid entrapment of the *Human* experience on *Earth.* It is meant to provide a *realization* of a simple truth—although much additional *fragmented* esoteric hype has been attached to it.

In *Lesson-5*, we introduced part of this technique using *imagined secondary viewpoints.* This time, we will be using the actual *planets* in this solar system—just as the ancient practice suggests. We will make a more literal exercise out of it, using the *physical planets* themselves, rather than *consider* anything esoteric about what they might symbolically represent.

This *process* is *run* repeatedly in series several times for each *"planet"* (*terminal*) listed: "EARTH"; "THE MOON"; "MERCURY"; "VENUS"; "MARS"; "JUPITER"; and "SATURN." Once you have practiced what is here to the point of an increased certainty on your *spiritual perception* (*ZU-Vision*), you can later apply additional steps from *"Locational-POV Processing"* in *Lesson-5* to advance this exercise further. [*Eyes closed; blindfolded if necessary.*]

A1. *"Be above ---; looking down at it."*

A2. *"Spot three points on the surface."*

B1. *"Be inside ---; occupying its center."*

B2. *"Spot three points interior to it."*

The next exercise is best practiced outdoors. It requires simply walking around; but as you do, focus on getting a sense that you are remaining in one position and moving the *Universe* beneath and around you. Then, add the earlier steps (from further above) of *"spotting objects"* and *"noticing the distance/space"* between you and them. After this is accomplished with ease, start to *alternate* between the idea of you *"moving through the Universe"* and *"moving the Universe around"* you (keeping with one idea for a few minutes before switching to the other).

To complete this lesson and *processing level*, we include several exercises that first appeared in the original *"Wizard Training Regimen"* outlined for the *Systemology Society* many years ago.

• With eyes closed: *Imagine* a *duplicate* (identical *facsimile-copy*) of your presently owned *"Human Body"* out in front of you. Make a copy next to it. And another. And several more. When you have about eight or so, push them together into a "ball" (or single *mass*) and *collapse it* into nothing. *Imagine* another *duplicate*. Make a copy next to it; and many more copies. Then push them together into a ball and toss it away. Continue this step until you feel more comfortable easily *creating (imagining mental imagery)* "bodies."

• With eyes closed: *Imagine* a *duplicate* of your present *body*, seeing it as "ideal" and "healthy." Then unmake it. Make it again; then unmake it. Repeat this several times.

• While looking into a mirror: *Get the sense* that there is "something there"; then *get the sense* that there is "nothing there." Alternate between these *considerations* repeatedly several times.

• With eyes closed: *Imagine* a busy or crowded place (mall, depot, or street corner). Decide to *be there* (place your *point-of-view* in a specific location). Look around and *spot* "terminals" (*objects* and *people*) and "*motion*" in the scenery. Practice this for multiple locations (preferably until there is an increase in actual perception).

• Use the location you like best from the previous exercise: *Imagine* making a *facsimile-copy* of your present "*Human Body*" to use as a *point-of-view* ("POV" or *viewpoint*). Then, unmake the *Body*, but remain in the location as an *Awareness*, continuing to look with your *point-of-view* there. Repeatedly alternate making and unmaking the *Body*, but still being able to "look out at" the surrounding scenery.

• Perform the previous exercise: *Imagine* a *facsimile-copy* of the *Body* out in front of you, but this time using a *point-of-view* "outside" the *Body* to look around at the location. Then use a *point-of-view* from "inside" the *Body* to look around at the location. Practice repeatedly alternating between these two *viewpoints*.

• Perform the previous exercise (in full), but this time adding: *Get the sense* of other persons acknowledging your presence when they are near (or walking by), even if they don't look at the *Body*.

• Select a basic solid "object/shape" (*pyramid, cone, cube, sphere, &tc.*) for practicing the four previous *locational* exercises as a cycle: *Imagine* using the *object* as your body; making and unmaking, alternating *viewpoints*, *spotting* other *terminals* and *motions*, and receiving acknowledgments ("*hellos*" *&tc.*) for your presence.

• Perform the previous exercise, but this time adding: unmaking the *Body/Shape* and *point-of-view* from one spot and making it again at other spots in the location. Also: *Get the sense* of moving the *Body/Shape* like a "playing piece" of a *game* (across a *game board*).

• Perform the previous *locational* exercises as a cycle; do this completely (as a complete *process*) for each of the following *"Body"* *terminals*: a duplicate of your *present body*; an *elderly body*; a *child's body*; a *different gendered-body* than your present one; a *sparkly-cloud* of *silvery-white energy* with small *golden balls for eyes* (as a *body*); and finally, using your *Awareness* as a *point-of-view* (with nothing added as a *body*).

The final exercise (below) requires the ability to *conceive of* or *maintain a sense of* "centering" or "focusing" your own *Awareness* as a *viewpoint* (or POV) a few feet *behind* the *head* of your present *body*. In addition to this, a *Seeker* should be able to *expand their perception of space* (as an *Awareness*) to include the *Body* from this "distance." This is a progress checkpoint on the *Pathway*. If this is above a *Seeker's* present *reality* and *ability*, than this is a suitable point to cycle back to the beginning of the *Professional Course* for an additional "pass."

Often, this *sense* of "operating from be-hind the head" is best practiced in a "public" place at first (because of the amount of *terminals* and *motion*), but it may also be practiced when performing your everyday routine (when it is safe and appropriate to do so). As a *systematic process*, it is best to allocate a specific peri-od of time for its actual "practice," al-though there are some *Seekers* that eventually find that they start to *know-ingly* operate in the mode more as they progress further along the *Pathway*.

In this practice: as you "walk the body" around a public place, you will still use its eyes for general spatial-orientation, but while *having a sense* that you are lar-ger than the *Body* and encompassing it from a few feet behind the head.

To further this practice: as you *observe* or *look* from a single stationary location; use the *body's eyes* to *spot* some *terminals*, then *spot* some *motions.* As you do this, *get the sense* that the *body's eyes* are sensing the *images/scenery* and sending this information to the *brain* and *control-center* of the *Body*—which, in turn, is *relaying* this "*communication*" along some kind of channel to *you* as the *Spiritual Awareness* behind the *Body.*

As an advanced step: attempt to *ignore the perceptions* received and relayed by the *Body,* whether eyes opened or closed, and *get a sense of* or *imagine* observing the *Body*—and surrounding *scenery* (*terminals* and *motions*)—using *only* your *viewpoint* as an *Awareness* behind the *Body.* Then alternating between this step and the previous *stationary location* step.

This completes *Systemology Level-4.*

*The Systemology Professional Course*
continues in the next lesson booklet:
**SPIRITUAL IMPLANTS**

# GLOSSARY

**actualization** : to make actual, not just potential; to bring into full solid Reality; to realize fully in *Awareness* as a "thing."

**agreement (reality)** : unanimity of opinion of what is "thought" to be known; an accepted arrangement of how things are; things we consider as "real" or as an "is" of "reality"; a consensus of what is real as made by standard-issue (common) participants; what an individual contributes to or accepts as "real"; in *Systemology*, a synonym for "*reality.*"

**alpha** : the first, primary, basic, superior or beginning of some form; in *Systemology*, referring to the state of existence operating on spiritual archetypes and postulates, will and intention "exterior" to the low-level condensation and solidarity of energy and matter as the 'physical universe' (*beta*).

**alpha-spirit** : a "spiritual" *Life*-form; the "true" *Self* or I-AM; the *individual*; the spiritual (*alpha*) *Self* that is animating the (*beta*) physical body or "*genetic vehicle*" using a continuous *Lifeline* of spiritual ("*ZU*") energy; an individual spiritual (*alpha*) entity possessing no physical mass or measurable waveform (motion) in the Physical Universe as itself, so it animates the (*beta*) physical body or "*genetic vehicle*" as a catalyst to experience *Self*-determined causality in effect within the *Physical Universe*; a singular unit or point of *Spiritual Awareness* that is *Aware* that it is *Aware*.

**alpha thought** : the highest spiritual *Self-determination* over creation and existence exercised by an Alpha-Spirit; the Alpha range of pure *Creative Ability* based on direct postulates and considerations of *Beingness*; spiritual qualities comparable to "thought" but originating in Alpha-existence, independently superior to a Mind-System.

**ascension** : actualized *Awareness* elevated to the point of true "spiritual existence" exterior to *beta existence*. An "Ascended Master" is one who has returned to an incarnation on Earth as an inherently *Enlightened One*, demonstrable in their words and actions; they have the ability to *Self-direct* the "Mind" and "Body" as *Self* (as a "Spirit"); and to maintain consciousness as a personal identity continuum with the same *Self-directed* control and communication of Will-Intention that is exercised, actualized and developed deliberately during one's present incarnation.

**associative knowledge** : significance or meaning of a facet or aspect assigned to (or considered to have) a direct relationship with another facet; to connect or relate ideas or facets of existence with one another; in traditional systems logic, an equivalency of significance or meaning between facets or sets that are grouped together, such as in $(a + b) + c = a + (b + c)$; in Systemology, erroneous associative knowledge is assignment of the same value to all facets or parts considered as related (even when they are not actually so), such as in $a = a,\ b = a,\ c = a$ and so forth without distinction.

**attention** : active use of *Awareness* toward a specific aspect or thing; the act of "attending" with the presence of *Self*; a direction of focus or concentration of *Awareness* along a particular channel or conduit or toward a particular terminal node or communication termination point; the Self-directed concentration of personal energy as a combination of observation, thought-waves and consideration; focused application of *Self-Directed Awareness*.

**awareness** : the highest sense of-and-as *Self* in knowing and being as I-AM (the *Alpha-Spirit*); the extent of beingness directed as a viewpoint (POV) experienced by *Self* as *Knowingness*.

**beta (awareness)** : all consciousness activity ("*Awareness*") in the "Physical Universe" (KI, in *Zuism*) or else in *beta-existence*; *Awareness* within the range of the *genetic-body*, including material thoughts, emotional responses and physical motors; personal *Awareness* of physical energy and physical matter moving through physical space and experienced as "time"; the *Awareness* held by *Self* that is restricted to an organic *Lifeform* or "*genetic vehicle*" in which it experiences causality in *beta-existence*.

**beta (existence)** : all manifestation in the "Physical Universe" (KI, in *Zuism*); the conditions of *Awareness* for the *Alpha-spirit* (*Self*) as a physical organic *Lifeform* or "*genetic vehicle*" in which it experiences causality in the *Physical Universe*.

**charge** : to fill or furnish with a quality; to supply with energy; to lay a command upon; in *Systemology*—to imbue with intention; to overspread with emotion; personal energy stores and significances entwined as fragmentation in mental images, reactive-response encoding and intellectual (and/or) programmed beliefs.

**channel** : a specific stream, course, current, direction or route; to form or cut a groove or ridge or otherwise guide along a specific course; a direct path; an artificial aqueduct created to connect two water bodies or water or make travel possible.

**circuit** : a circular path or loop; a closed-path within a system that allows a flow; a pattern or action or wave movement that follows a specific route or potential path only; in *Systemology*, "*communication processing*" pertaining to a specific *flow* of energy or information along a channel; "*feedback loop.*"

**communication** : successful transmission of information, data, energy (&tc.) along a message line, with a reception of feedback; an energetic flow of intention to cause an effect (or duplication) at a distance; the personal energy moved or acted upon by will or else 'selective directed attention'; the 'messenger action' used to transmit and receive energy across a medium; also relay of energy, a message or signal—or even locating a personal POV (viewpoint) for the Self—along the *ZU-line*.

**condense (condensation)** : the transition of vapor to liquid; denoting a change in state to a more substantial or solid condition; leading to a more compact or solid form.

**confront** : to come around in front of; to be in the presence of; to stand in front of, or in the face of; to meet "face-to-face" or "face-up-to"; additionally, in *Systemology*, to fully tolerate or acceptably withstand an encounter with a particular manifestation without an automatic reactive response.

**consideration** : careful analytical reflection of all aspects; deliberation; determining the significance of a "thing" in relation to similarity or dissimilarity to other "things"; evaluation of facts and importance of certain facts; thorough examination of all aspects related to, or important for, making a decision; the analysis of consequences and estimation of significance when making decisions; also in *Systemology*, the *postulate* or *Alpha-Thought* that defines the state of *beingness* for what something "*is.*"

**defragmentation** : the *reparation* of wholeness; collecting all dispersed parts to reform an original whole; a process of removing "*fragmentation*" in data or knowledge to provide a clear understanding; applying techniques and processes that promote a *holistic* interconnected *alpha* state, favoring observational *Awareness* of continuity in all spiritual and physical systems; in *Systemology*, a "*Seeker*" achieving actualized "*Self-Honest Awareness*" is said to be in a basic state of *beta-defragmentation*, whereas *Alpha-defragmentation* is the rehabilitation of the *creative ability*, managing the *Spiritual Timeline* and the POV of *Self* as Alpha-Spirit (I-AM).

**existence** : the *state* or fact of *apparent manifestation*; the resulting combination of the Principles of Manifestation: consciousness, motion and substance; continued *survival*; that which independently exists.

**exterior** : outside of; on the outside; in *Systemology*, we mean specifically the POV of *Self* that is *'outside of'* the *Human Condition,* free of the physical and mental trappings of the Physical Universe; a metahuman range of consideration; see also *'Zu-Vision'*.

**external** : a force coming from outside; information received from outside sources; in *Systemology*, the objective *'Physical Universe'* existence, or *beta-existence*, that the Physical Body or *genetic vehicle* is essentially *anchored* to for its considerations of locational space-time as a dimension or POV.

**fragmentation** : breaking into parts and scattering the pieces; the *fractioning* of wholeness or the *fracture* of a holistic interconnected *alpha* state, favoring observational *Awareness* of perceived connectivity between parts; *discontinuity*; separation of a totality into parts; in *Systemology*, a person outside of *Self-Honesty* is said to be operating from a *fragmented* state.

**flow** : movement across (or through) a channel (or conduit); a direction of active energetic motion, typically distinguished as either an *in-flow*, *out-flow* or *cross-flow*.

**genetic-vehicle** : a physical *Life*-form; the physical (*beta*) body that is animated/controlled by the (*Alpha*) *Spirit* using a continuous *Spiritual Lifeline* (ZU); a physical (*beta*) organic receptacle and catalyst for the (*Alpha*) *Self* to operate "causes" and experience "effects" within the *Physical Universe*.

**harmful-act** : a counter-survival mode of behavior or action (esp. that causes harm to one of more *Spheres of Existence*)—or—an overtly aggressive (hostile and/or destructive) action against an individual or any other *Sphere of Existence*; in *Utilitarian Systemology*—a short-sighted (serves fewest/lowest *Spheres of Existence*) intentional overtly harmful action to resolve a perceived problem; a revision of the rule for standard *Utilitarianism* for Systemology to distinguish actions which provide the least benefit to the least number of *Spheres of Existence*, or else the greatest harm to the greatest number of *Spheres of Existence*; in *moral philosophy*—an action which can be experienced by few and/or which one would not be willing to experience for themselves (*theft, slander, rape, &tc*); an iniquity or iniquitous act.

**hold-back** : withheld communications (esp. actions) such as "*Hold-Outs*"; intentional (or automatic) withdrawal (as opposed to reach); Self-restraint (which may eventually be enforced or automated); not reaching, acting or expressing, when one should be; an ability that is now restrained (on automatic) due to inability to withhold it on Self-determinism alone.

**hold-outs** : in photography, the numerous snapshots/pictures withheld from the final display or professional presentation of the event; withheld communications; in Utilitarian Systemology—energetic withdrawal and communication breaks with a "*terminal*" and its *Sphere of Existence* as a result of a "*Harmful-Act*"; unspoken or undiscovered (hidden, covert) actions that an individual withholds communications of, fearing punishment or endangerment of *Self-preservation* (*First Sphere*); the act of hiding (or keeping hidden) the truth of a "*Harmful-Act*"; a refusal to communicate with a *Pilot*; also "*Hold-Back.*"

**holistic** : the examination of interconnected systems as encompassing something greater than the *sum* of their "parts."

**Human Condition** : a standard default state of Human experience that is generally accepted to be the extent of its potential identity (*beingness*) —currently treated as *Homo Sapiens Sapiens,* but which is scheduled for replacement by *Homo Novus* (the "New Human").

**imagination** : ability to create *mental imagery* in one's Personal Universe at will and change or alter it as desired; the ability to create, change and dissolve mental images on command or as an act of will; to create a mental image or have associated imagery displayed (or "conjured") in the mind that may or may not be treated as real (or memory recall) and may or may not accurately duplicate objective reality; to employ *creative abilities* of the Spirit that are independent of reality agreements with beta-existence.

**imprint** : to strongly impress, stamp, mark (or outline) onto a softer 'impressible' substance; to mark with pressure onto a surface; in *Systemology*, used to indicate permanent Reality impressions marked by frequencies, energies or interactions experienced during periods of emotional distress, pain, unconsciousness, loss, enforcement, or something antagonistic to physical (personal) survival, all of which are are stored with other reactive response-mechanisms at lower-levels of *Awareness* as opposed to the active memory database and proactive processing center of the Mind; an experiential "memory-set" that may later resurface—be triggered or stimulated artificially—as Reality, of which similar responses will be engaged automatically; holographic-like imagery "stamped" onto consciousness as composed of energetic *facets* tied to the "snap-shot" of an experience.

**imprinting incident** : the first or original event

instance communicated and *emotionally encoded* onto an individual's "*Spiritual Timeline*" (recorded memory from all lifetimes), which formed a permanent impression that is later used to mechanistically treat future contact on that channel; the first or original occurrence of some particular *facet* or mental image related to a certain type of *encoded response*, such as pain and discomfort, losses and victimization, and even the acts that we have taken against others along the *Spiritual Timeline* of our existence that caused them to also be *Imprinted*.

**intention** : directed application of Will; to intend (have "in Mind") or signify (give "significance" to) for or toward a particular purpose; in *Systemology* (from the *Standard Model*)—the spiritual activity at WILL (5.0) directed by an *Alpha Spirit* (7.0); the application of WILL as "Cause" from a higher order of Alpha Thought and consideration (6.0).

**interior** : inside of; on the inside; in *Systemology*, we mean specifically the POV of *Self* that is fixed to the *'internal' Human Condition,* including the *Reactive Control Center* (RCC) and Mind-System or *Master Control Center* (MCC); within *beta-existence*.

**internal** : a force coming from inside; information received from inside sources; in *Systemology*, the objective experience of *beta-existence* associated with the Physical Body or *genetic vehicle* and its POV regarding sensation and perception; from inside the body; in the body.

**invalidate** : decrease the level or degree or *agreement* as Reality.

**mental image** : a subjectively experienced "picture" created and imagined into being by the Alpha-Spirit (or at lower levels, one of its automated mechanisms) that includes all perceptible *facets* of totally immersive scene, which may be forms originated by an individual, or a "facsimile-copy" ("snap-shot") of something seen or encountered; a duplication of wave-forms in one's Personal Universe as a "picture" that mirror an "external" Universe experience, such as an *Imprint*.

**perception** : internalized processing of data received by the *senses*; to become *Aware of* via the senses.

**pilot** : a professional steersman responsible for healthy functional operation of a ship toward a specific destination; in *Systemology*, an intensive trained individual qualified to specially apply *Systemology Processing* to assist other *Seekers* on the *Pathway*.

**point-of-view (POV)** : a point to view from; an opinion or attitude as expressed from a specific identity-phase; a specific standpoint or vantage-point; a definitive manner of consideration specific to an individual phase or identity; a place or position affording a specific view or vantage; circumstances and programming of an individual that is conducive to a particular response, consideration or belief-set (paradigm); a position (consideration) or place (location) that provides a specific view or perspective (subjective) on experience (of the objective).

**postulate** : to put forward as truth; to suggest or assume an existence *to be*; to state or affirm the existence of particular conditions; to provide a basis of reasoning and belief; a basic theory accepted as fact; in *Systemology*, Alpha-Thought —the top-most decisions or considerations made by the Alpha-Spirit regarding the "*is-ness*" (what things "are") about energy-matter and space-time.

**presence** : a quality of some thing (*energy/matter*) being "present" in space-time; personal orientation of *Self* as an *Awareness* (*POV*) located in present space-time (environment) and communicating with extant energy-matter.

**processing command line (PCL)** : a directed input; a specific command using highly selective language for *Systemology Processing*; a predetermined directive statement (cause) intended to focus concentrated attention (effect).

**processing, systematic** : the inner-workings or "through-put" result of systems; in *Systemology*, a method of applied spiritual technology used toward personal Self-Actualization; methods of selective directed attention, communicated language and associative imagery that increases personal control of the human condition.

**realization** : the clear perception of an understanding; a consideration or understanding on what is "actual"; to make "real" or give "reality" to so as to grant a property of "beingness" or "being as it is"; the state or instance of coming to an *Awareness*; in *Systemology*, "gnosis" or true knowledge achieved during *systematic processing*; achievement of a new (or higher) cognition, true knowledge or perception of Self; a consideration of reality or assignment of meaning.

**responsibility** : the *ability* to *respond*; the extent of mobilizing *power* and *understanding* an individual maintains as *Awareness* to enact *change*; the proactive ability to *Self-direct* and make decisions independent of an outside authority.

**Seeker** : an individual on the *Pathway to Self-Honesty*; a practitioner of *Mardukite Systemology* or *Systemology Processing*, that is working toward *Spiritual Ascension*.

**Self-actualization** : bringing the full potential of the Human spirit into Reality; expressing full capabilities and creativeness of the *Alpha-Spirit*.

**Self-determinism** : the freedom to act, clear of external control or influence; the personal control of Will to direct intention.

**Self-honesty** : the basic or original *alpha* state of *being* and *knowing*; clear and present total *Awareness* of-and-as *Self*, in its most basic and true proactive expression of itself as *Spirit* or *I-AM*—free of artificial attachments, perceptive filters and other emotionally-reactive or mentally-conditioned programming imposed on the human condition by the systematized physical world; the ability to experience existence without judgment.

**spiritual timeline** : a continuous stream of moment-to-moment *Mental Images* (or a record of experiences) that defines the "past" of a spiritual being (or *Alpha-Spirit*) and which includes impressions (*imprints, &tc.*) from all life-incarnations and significant spiritual events the being has encountered; in Systemology, also "*backtrack.*"

**Spheres of Existence** : a series of *eight* concentric circles, rings or spheres (each larger than the former) that is overlaid onto the Standard Model of Beta-Existence to demonstrate the dynamic systems of existence extending out from the POV of Self (often as a "body") at the *First Sphere*; these are given in the basic eightfold systems as: *Self, Home/Family, Groups, Humanity, Life on Earth, Physical Universe, Spiritual Universe* and *Infinity-Divinity.*

**Systemology** : a modern tradition of applied religious philosophy and spiritual technology based on *Arcane Tablets* (in combination with *"general systemology"* and *"games theory"*) developed in the New Age underground by Joshua Free in 2011 as an advanced futurist extension of the *Mardukite Research Org.*

**terminal (node)** : a point, end, or mass, on a line; a connection point for closing an electric circuit, such as a post on a battery terminating at each end of its own systematic function; a point of connectivity with other points; in systems, a contact point of interaction; a point of interaction with other points.

**turbulence** : a quality or state of distortion or disturbance that creates irregularity of a flow or pattern; the quality or state of aberration on a line (such as ragged edges) or the emotional "turbulent feelings" attached to a particular flow or terminal node; a violent, haphazard or disharmonious commotion (such as in the ebb of gusts and lulls of wind action).

**validation** : a reinforcement of agreements or considerations as being "real."

**viewpoint** : see *"point-of-view" (POV)*.

**willingness** : the state of conscious Self-determined ability and interest (directed attention) to *Be*, *Do* or *Have*; a Self-determined consideration to reach, face up to (*confront*) or manage some "mass" or energy; the extent to which an individual considers themselves able to participate, act or communicate along some line, to put attention or intention on the line, or to produce (create) an effect.

***ZU*** : the ancient Sumerian cuneiform sign for the archaic verb—*"to know," "knowingness"* or *"awareness"*; in *Mardukite Zuism and Systemology*, the active energy/matter of the "Spiritual Universe" (AN) experienced as a *Lifeforce* or *consciousness* that imbues living forms extant in the "Physical Universe" (KI); *"Spiritual Life Energy"*; energy demonstrated by the WILL of an actualized *Alpha-Spirit* in the "Spiritual Universe" (AN), which impinges its *Awareness* into the Physical Universe (KI), animating/controlling *Life* for its experience of *beta-existence* along an individual Alpha-Spirit's personal *Identity-continuum*, called a *ZU-line*.

***Zu*-Line** : a theoretical construct in *Mardukite Zuism and Systemology* demonstrating *Spiritual*

*Life Energy* (*ZU*) as a personal individual "continuum" of Awareness interacting with all Spheres of Existence on the Standard Model of Systemology; a spectrum of potential variations and interactions of a monistic continuum or singular *Spiritual Life Energy* demonstrated on the Standard Model; an energetic channel of potential POV and "locations" of Beingness, demonstrated in early Systemology materials as an individual Alpha-Spirit's personal *Identity- continuum*, potentially connecting *Awareness* of *Self* with "*Infinity*" simultaneous with all points considered in existence; a symbolic demonstration of the "*Life-line*" on which *Awareness (ZU)* extends from the direction of the "Spiritual Universe" (AN) in its true original *alpha state* through an entire possible range of activity resulting in its *beta state* and control of a *genetic-entity* occupying the *Physical Universe (KI).*

**Zu-Vision** : the true and basic (*Alpha*) Point-of-View (perspective, POV) maintained by *Self* as *Alpha-Spirit* outside boundaries or considerations of the *Human Condition* and *exterior* to beta-existence reality agreements with the Physical Universe; a POV of Self *as* "a unit of Spiritual Awareness" that exists independent of a "body" and entrapment in a *Human Condition*; "spirit vision" in its truest sense.

*explore the*
## Fundamentals of Systemology
*in six*
Basic Course Lesson Booklets

Also
available
as a
*six-in-one*
hardcover
edition!

# THE SYSTEMOL

Seekers and students of the *Basic Course* and *Professional Course* will also be interested in the *Systemology Core Research Series*. These eight volumes are a complete chronological record of the Mardukite New Thought developments from the Systemology Society, published in 2019 through 2023.

The *Systemology Core* begins with the first professional publication released when the *Mardukite Systemology Society* emerged from the underground in 2019, with: *"The Tablets of Destiny Revelation."*

# OGY PATHWAY

**The Tablets of Destiny Revelation:**
*How Long-Lost Anunnaki Wisdom
Can Change the Fate of Humanity*

**Crystal Clear:** *Handbook for Seekers*

**Metahuman Destinations** (*2 volumes*)

**Imaginomicon:**
*Approaching Gateways to Higher Universes*

**Way of the Wizard:** *Utilitarian Systemology*

**Systemology-180:** *Fast-Track to Ascension*

**Systemology Backtrack:**
*Reclaiming Spiritual Power & Past-Life Memory*

PUBLISHED BY THE **JOSHUA FREE** IMPRINT REPRESENTING

**The Mardukite Academy of Systemology**

**mardukite.com**

www.ingramcontent.com/pod-product-compliance
Lightning Source LLC
Chambersburg PA
CBHW071211120626
46546CB00006B/2512